# Charles & Diana's GUIDE FOR A Happy, Loving Marriage

An "Unwritten Classics" Book
*Published by Carol Publishing Group*

Copyright © 1995 by Carol Publishing Group
All rights reserved. No part of this book may be reproduced or transmitted in any form, except by a newspaper or magazine reviewer who wishes to quote brief passages in connections with a review.

An "Unwritten Classics" Book
Published by Carol Publishing Group
"Unwritten Classics" is a registered trademark of Carol Communications, Inc.
Editorial Offices: 600 Madison Avenue, New York, N.Y. 10022
Sales and Distribution Offices: 120 Enterprise Avenue, Secaucus, N.J. 07094
In Canada: Canadian Manda Group, One Atlantic Avenue, Suite 105, Toronto, Ontario, M6K 3E7
Queries regarding rights and permission should be addressed to Carol Publishing Group, 600 Madison Avenue, New York, N.Y. 10022

Carol Publishing Group books are available at special discounts for bulk purchases, sales promotion, fund-raising, or educational purposes. Special editions can be created to specifications. For details, contact: Special Sales Department, Carol Publishing Group, 120 Enterprise Avenue, Secaucus, N.J. 07094

Manufactured in the United States of America
10 9 8 7 6 5 4 3 2 1

ISBN 0-8216-1002-3